Audubon's Birds of America Coloring Book

John James Audubon

Rendered for Coloring by
PAUL E. KENNEDY

Dover Publications, Inc., New York

PUBLISHER'S NOTE

Forty-six different species of birds from all parts of the United States are included in this book. The pictures have been faithfully redrawn by Paul E. Kennedy from originals by John James Audubon (1785–1851), the most famous American painter-naturalist. The original hand-colored illustrations were first published in his classic work *The Birds of America* (folio edition 1827–1838; octavo edition 1840–1844).

For each species, the caption supplies the modern common and scientific names and the current range (by general region). No distinction is made between breeding range and winter range. Only the area of the United States, exclusive of Alaska and Hawaii, is considered. The birds shown are usually adult males when the caption does not give information on age and sex.

Audubon's original plates, numbered to correspond to the pages of the book, have been reproduced in color on the covers. If you follow them, you will not only have a great deal of coloring pleasure, but you will also learn how to identify many important birds.

Published in Canada by General Publishing Company, Ltd.,
30 Lesmill Road, Don Mills, Toronto, Ontario.
Published in the United Kingdom by Constable and Company, Ltd.,
10 Orange Street, London WC 2.

Audubon's Birds of America Coloring Book is a new work, first published by Dover Publications, Inc., in 1974. The line renderings, based on colored illustrations in *The Birds of America* by John James Audubon (published by Audubon and J. B. Chevalier in 1840–1844), were prepared specially for the present edition by Paul E. Kennedy.

DOVER *Pictorial Archive* SERIES

International Standard Book Number: 0-486-23049-X

Manufactured in the United States of America
Dover Publications, Inc.
180 Varick Street
New York, N.Y. 10014

1 American Avocet (*Recurvirostra americana*). West of the Mississippi. Head and neck pinkish tan in breeding season.

2   Red-winged Blackbird *(Agelaius phoeniceus)*. Throughout United States.
Above: adult male. Below: young male (left) and female.

3   Eastern Bluebird *(Sialia sialis)*. East, Plains, Arizona. Above: male. Below: female feeding young.

4   Painted Bunting *(Passerina ciris)*. South. Top: female (the others are males).

5   Cardinal *(Richmondena cardinalis)*. East, Southwest. Above: male. Below: female.

6   Yellow-breasted Chat *(Icteria virens).* Throughout United States. The female is in the nest; the others are male.

7   Whooping Crane *(Grus americana)*. Texas (Aransas National Wildlife
     Refuge) .

8   White-winged Crossbill *(Loxia leucoptera)*. Far Northern states. The top-most bird and the partly hidden one are females, the others males.

9   Mourning Dove (*Zenaidura macroura*). Throughout United States. The
bird in the nest and the one at top left are females, the others males.

10   Wood Duck *(Aix sponsa)*. East, Northwest. The bird in the log and the one at top right are females, the others males.

11   Snowy Egret *(Leucophoyx thula)*. Southeast, Southwest.

12   Purple Finch (*Carpodacus purpureus*). Northeast, West Coast. The bottom bird is a female.

13   American Flamingo (*Phoenicopterus ruber*). Florida.

14   Yellow-shafted Flicker *(Colaptes auratus)*. East, Plains. The bottom bird is a male.

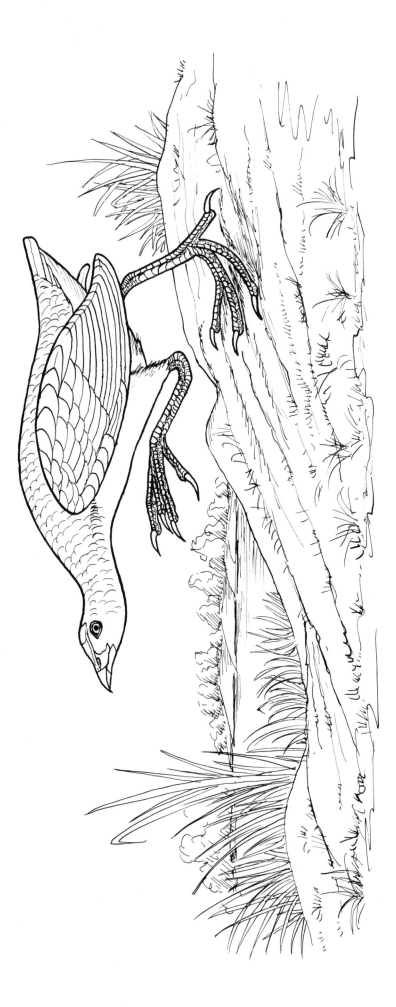

15   Purple Gallinule (*Porphyrula martinica*). Deep South.

16   American Goldfinch *(Spinus tristis)*. Throughout United States. Above:
male. Below: female.

17   Evening Grosbeak *(Hesperiphona vespertina).* Northeast, West. From top
to bottom: adult male, female, young male.

18   Rose-breasted Grosbeak *(Pheucticus ludovicianus)*. Northeast, North Central states. Top: young male. Center: female. Below: two males.

19   Sparrow Hawk *(Falco sparverius)*. Throughout United States.

20   Great Blue Heron (*Ardea herodias*). Throughout United States.

21   Ruby-throated Hummingbird *(Archilochus colubris)*. East, Plains. Two males are at the top left, a female at top right, a young bird on the nest.

22   Blue Jay *(Cyanocitta cristata)*. East, Plains. The bird with outspread wings is a male.

23   Belted Kingfisher (*Megaceryle alcyon*). Throughout United States. The bird with the fish is a female.

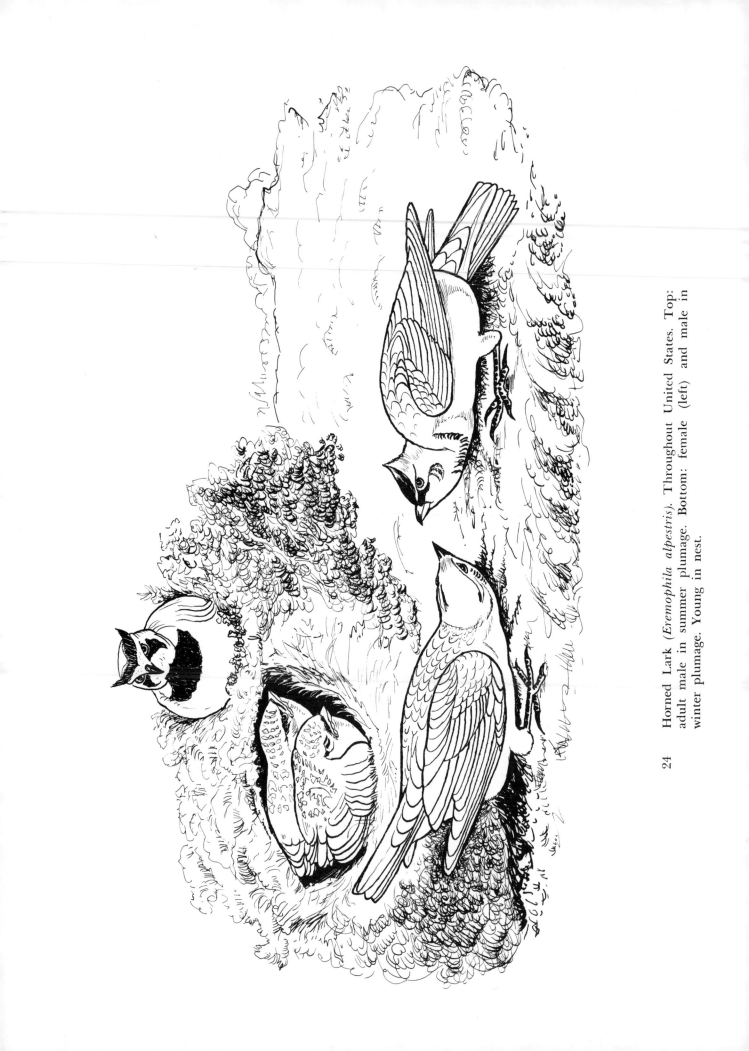

24 Horned Lark (*Eremophila alpestris*). Throughout United States. Top: adult male in summer plumage. Bottom: female (left) and male in winter plumage. Young in nest.

25   Mallard (*Anas platyrhynchos*). Throughout United States. The bird with the open bill and the one with its bill on the water are females.

26   Eastern Meadowlark *(Sturnella magna).* East, Southwest. The flying bird and the standing one are males, the others females.

27   Hooded Merganser (*Lophodytes cucullatus*). East, Northwest. The male is at the left.

28   Baltimore Oriole *(Icterus galbula)*. East, Plains. Top: adult male. A
young male is on the nest, a female on the twig.

29   Screech Owl *(Otus asio)*. Throughout United States.

30   Snowy Owl (*Nyctea scandiaca*). Northwest.

31   Brown Pelican (*Pelecanus occidentalis*). Southern and Western coasts.

32   American Redstart *(Setophaga ruticilla).* East, North Central states. The female is above.

33   Robin *(Turdus migratorius)*. Throughout United States. The adult male
has the insect, the adult female the berry.

34   Fox Sparrow (*Passerella iliaca*). Southeast, West. The male is at the right.

35   White-throated Sparrow *(Zonotrichia albicollis)*. East, South. The male is below.

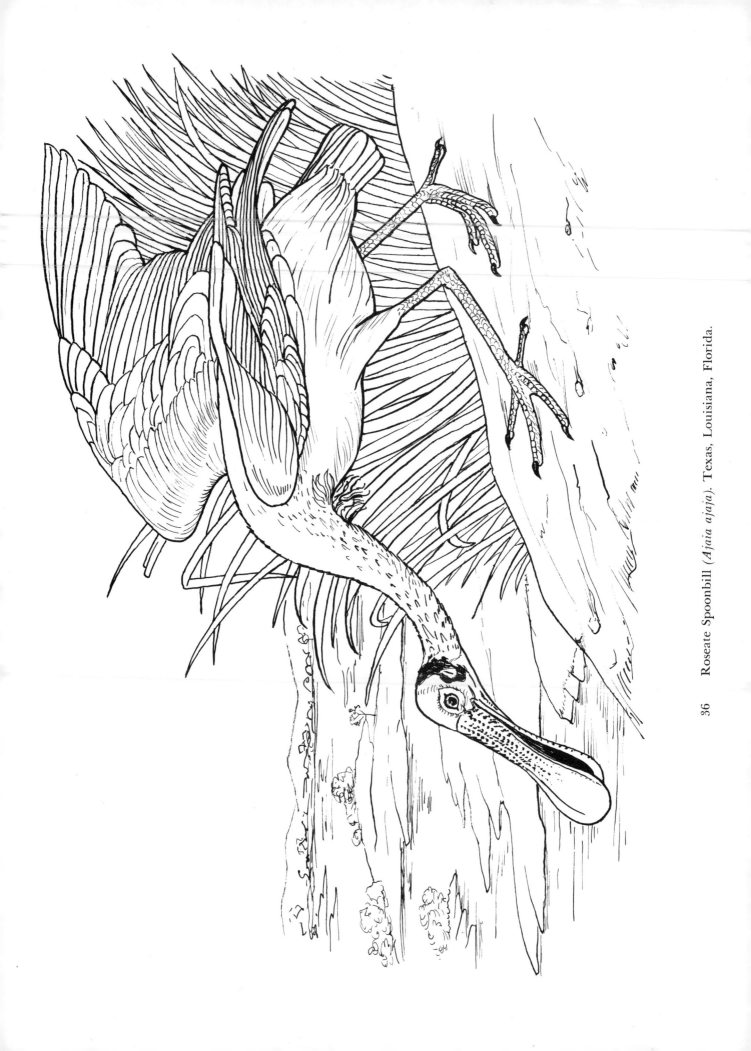

36   Roseate Spoonbill (*Ajaia ajaja*). Texas, Louisiana, Florida.

37   Scarlet Tanager *(Piranga olivacea).* East. The male is above.

38   Brown Thrasher *(Toxostoma rufum)*. East, Plains. The lowest bird is a female.

39   Rufous-sided Towhee *(Pipilo erythrophthalmus).* Throughout United States. The male is above.

40 Turkey *(Meleagris gallopavo)*. Southeast, Southwest.

41 Blackburnian Warbler *(Dendroica fusca)*. Northeast. The male is at the left.

42   Canada Warbler (*Wilsonia canadensis*). Northeast. The male is above.

43　　Cerulean Warbler *(Dendroica cerulea)*. Northeast, North Central states.
Above: adult male. Below: young male.

44   Chestnut-sided Warbler *(Dendroica pensylvanica)*. Northeast. The male is at the left.

45   Whip-poor-will (*Caprimulgus vociferus*). East, Southwest.

46   Pileated Woodpecker *(Dryocopus pileatus)*. East, Northwest. Top: female.
Center: male. Bottom: two young males.